Samuel Swaim Stewart

Complete American Banjo School

Samuel Swaim Stewart

Complete American Banjo School

ISBN/EAN: 9783744650557

Printed in Europe, USA, Canada, Australia, Japan

Cover: Foto ©Lupo / pixelio.de

More available books at **www.hansebooks.com**

36th EDITION.

THE COMPLETE AMERICAN BANJO SCHOOL.

BY

S. S. STEWART.

***

PART FIRST:
Price, $2.00.

***

| PART FIRST, $2.00. | BOTH PARTS |
| PART SECOND, $2.00. | IN CLOTH, $5.00. |

PHILADELPHIA, PENNA.

PUBLISHED BY S. S. STEWART, No. 223 CHURCH ST.

☞ SEND FOR ILLUSTRATED CATALOGUE.

Copyright, 1887, by S. S. STEWART.

S. S. Stewart.

THE COMPLETE AMERICAN BANJO SCHOOL

PART I.

CONTENTS.

CONCERT PITCH AND GENERAL REMARKS	3
THE BANJO HEAD, THE BANJO STRINGS, THE FINGERBOARD	4
RUDIMENTS OF MUSIC	5
THE SCALES EXPLAINED	6
NATURAL SCALE OF THE BANJO with illustrations	7
BARRE CHORDS EXPLAINED	8
CHROMATIC SCALE AND EXERCISES ON THE SAME	9
EXERCISES IN TIME from number 1 to 13,	9 to 12
THE TWENTY FOUR SCALES AND CHORDS	13 to 15
TONIC CHORDS OF 24 KEYS	16
EXERCISES IN RAPID SHIFTING numbers 1, 2, 3, 4 and 5	17
EXERCISES IN WALTZ MOVEMENT numbers 1 to 6	18 and 19
EXERCISES IN MODULATION AND EXPRESSION	20 and 21
THE TREMOLO MOVEMENT, with Exercises	22 and 23
DRUM CHORDS	24
ARPEGGIO CHORDS	24
EXERCISES IN "BASS TUNED TO B"	25
VIBRATION AND "SNAP" SLURS EXPLAINED	25
VIBRATION SCHOTTISCHE WITH EXPLANATIONS	26
STACCATO AND LEGATO MOVEMENTS	26
FOUR EXERCISES IN VIBRATION TRILLING	27
THE HARMONIC TONES WITH EXPLANATIONS	28
EMBELLISHMENTS AND GRACE NOTES	29
EXERCISES IN VARIOUS KEYS WITH EXPLANATIONS	30, 31, 32
STROKE PLAYING EXPLAINED, with Exercises	33 and 34
THE "ROLL" IN STROKE PLAYING, with Exercises	35 and 36
MODULATIONS	37
THE DOMINANT CHORDS	38
TRANSPOSITION	39 and 40
DARKEYS PASSTIME (minor Jig) with Explanations	41
HOME SWEET HOME, with Explanations	41
MISCELLANEOUS EXERCISES ON DIFFERENT MOVEMENTS	42 to 45
SONG ACCOMPANIMENTS,	46 to 49
EMBELLISHMENT AND CADENZA EXERCISES	50

Copyright 1888 by S. S. Stewart.

The Complete American Banjo School.

PART 1st.

The Banjo is an instrument of very ancient origin, but only of late years has it become a perfected and favorite musical instrument.

*The Modern Banjo has five strings, the fifth being one quarter shorter than the others. The strings are manipulated by the fingers of the right hand, the left hand fingers being used to stop the string at various positions upon the fingerboard.

There are two distinct styles of manipulating the strings, known as the picking or Guitar style, and the stroke, or original Banjo style.

In picking, the small finger of right hand should rest upon the head, near the bridge.

The silver string and short string are struck with the thumb; the third string is picked with first finger, the second string with second finger and the first string with third finger.

In stroke playing, the thumb and first finger are used only. A thimble of german silver covers the nail of the finger. For fine execution this style is most obsolete but of great practical utility in playing some marches etc.

RELATIVE TO CONCERT PITCH.

(See pages 28 and 29 of "Observations on the Banjo.")

Years ago, when music was first printed for the Banjo, the natural keys of the Banjo were noted as A and E Major. At the present time we find the impracticability of this notation, as no Banjo is tuned in the pitch in which its music is noted; this fact alone is of no moment, for neither the B♭ or E♭ Cornets sound their tones as noted, nor do Clarinets. The main objection to the notation is because the pupil is taught in the keys of two, three or four sharps before he has learned to play in the natural key of C.

The reason the Banjo was noted in the keys in which it is presumed to be because long ago the instrument was strung with heavy strings like the Guitar, and was also of large size. By increasing the thickness of a string we produce the same effect as by lengthening the string.ˣHence Banjos strung with thick strings were tuned lower than Banjos of the present day which are strung much thinner. The Banjo was thus an instrument of sixteen feet tone, sounding an octave lower than the notes indicated.

The Guitar, Banjo and all other instruments as well as the male voice, which sound

---

* See Book "The Banjo" by the author _ also his lecture, "The Banjo Philosophically."
ˣ Not the same musical effect, but as regards pitch only.

an octave lower than written are said to be of sixteen feet tone. All instruments which register their tones as written are said to be of eight feet tone etc —. (A pipe in any simple wind instrument, or organ pipe, of about eight feet in length, gives the great C; the deepest and therefore in this respect, the normal tone of the key board of the organ. A pipe twice as long sounds an octave deeper, whilst a pipe only half as long sounds an octave higher) Hence the singularity of the expression is explained.

THE BANJO HEAD.
(See "Observations on the Banjo," page 22.)

The head of the Banjo should be of calf=skin and neither too thick nor too thin but of a happy medium. The head should be kept well strained and a skin that will not pull tight without breaking had best be broke at once and replaced by one that will stand. Damp weather will cause a tight head to become slack to a certain degree whilst too great heat will contract it, and often to such a degree as to split it. Therefore avoid keeping the instrument either in too hot or damp place.

THE STRINGS.
(See "Observations," page 18.)

Be careful to choose good strings and as nearly as possible of even thickness. The first and fifth strings should be of the same thickness. The second strings should be a little thicker than the first and the third string should be considerably thicker than the second. The fourth string should be of silk spun with silver plated copper wire. Good strings can not be told by their color the best and only sure way is to try them. False strings are frequently met with _that is strings which are not true in tone. These strings had best be discarded as they draw the inspiration out of any player. Often a string may sound fairly, open, but false when stopped at different frets or positions. This is caused by uneven thickness or density.

THE FINGERBOARD.
("See page 21 of Observations.")

The Banjo fingerboard should be perfectly level. It should be divided off into fretted positions. Raised frets, which are of very ancient origin upon stringed instruments, are not recommended for the Banjo, as they produce a metalic clanky tone and interfere with the rapid shifting of the hand.

Music for the Banjo or for any other instrument is written upon and between five parallel lines called a stave. Music is written in signs called notes and are named after the first seven letters of the alphabet; A. B. C D E F G.

When notes exceed the compass of the stave we add short lines called ledger lines. The following is the scale or gamut of the Banjo, with ledger lines above and below the stave.

A sign is placed at the beginning of the stave which is called the Treble or G Cleff. There are two Cleffs in common use, the Treble and Bass. Banjo music is always noted in the Treble Cleff.

The notes on the lines are named as follow:

The notes in the spaces, between the lines, are named as follow:

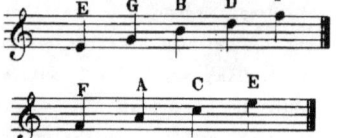

VALUE OF NOTES AND RESTS DURATION OF TIME Etc.

A whole note is equal in time to two half notes, four quarter notes, eight eighth notes etc. Thirty two thirty second notes would be played in the same time as one whole note. Each note has its corresponding rest — which is expressed as follows.

If a note or rest has a dot placed after it its duration is prolonged one half of its original value.

TRIPLETS.

When three notes are united, with the figure three, (3) as follow, it is called a triplet. The three notes are to be executed in the same time as two notes of the same kind.

A sharp (♯) raises a note one semitone or half tone.

A double sharp raises a note two semitones, or a full tone (𝄪)

A flat (♭) lowers a note a half tone. A double flat lowers a note two half tones or a full tone. (♭♭)

The sharps or flats which belong to any Key are marked at the signature or after the cleff. They effect all the notes of the same name in the piece unless contradicted by naturals. A natural (♮) contradicts either a flat or a sharp and restores the note to its original pitch.

But a double sharp is restored by a natural followed by a sharp. A double flat is restored by a natural followed by a flat.

THE SCALES.
(See "Observations," page 24.)

There are two kinds of scales the diatonic and the chromatic. The diatonic scale consists of five full tones and two semitones.

A semitone (half tone) is the smallest interval used in modern music.

The diatonic scale is divided in two classes. The Major and Minor.

The Major scales are the same ascending and descending (see scales further on).

The Minor scales not the same ascending and descending. The melodic Minor scale is formed with a view to melody and is written thus. In ascending the smaller intervals are from 2 to 3 and 7 to 8. In descending the smaller intervals are from 6 to 5 and from 3 to 2. (see Minor scales)

Every major key has a relative minor key and as there are twelve major keys there are in all twenty four keys. The relative minor key to any major key is always a third below it or a sixth above. A key is said to be minor when the third note in the scale is the distance of three semitones from the first note: or when the third note is one semitone flatter than in the major scale.

THE NATURAL SCALE OF THE BANJO.

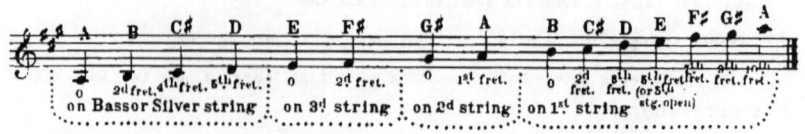

The above scale is written in its most simple manner. We now analyze the same and show the pupil that many notes of the same name and same degree upon the staff may be made upon different strings and in different positions upon the fingerboard.

We will now take each note of the foregoing scale separately and show each position where it maybe found upon the Banjo.

These four notes are made only on the 4th string at frets indicated.

This note is made on the 3d string open and also on the 4th string at 7th fret.

This note is made on 3d string 2d fret and on 4th string 9th fret.

This note is made on 2d string open and 3d string 4th fret and on 4th string 11th fret.

This note is made on 2d string 1st fret and 3d string 5th fret and on 4th string 12th fret. It is one octave above the note first started on in the scale.

This note is made on the first string, open 2d string 3d fret — 3d string 7th fret and on the 4th string 14th fret.

This note is made on the 1st string 2d fret — 2d string 5th fret, 3d string 9th fret and 4th string 16th fret.

This note is made on 1st string 3d fret, 2d string 6th fret, 3d string 10th fret, 4th string 17th fret.

This note is made on the first string 5th fret, — 2d string 8th fret, — 3d string 12th fret — 4th string 19th fret and also the 5th string open.

This note is made on the first string 7th fret 2d string 10th fret, 3d string 14th fret, 4th string 21st fret.

This note is made on 1st string 9th fret — 2d string 12th fret 3d string 16th fret and on 4th string 23d fret (on the head).

This note is found on 1st string 10th fret — 2d string 13th fret — 3d string 17th fret 4th string 24th fret (or on the head.)

BARRÉ CHORDS.

(See "Observations," page 2.)

Certain chords upon the Banjo are produced by what is termed the Barré,— which consists of placing the first finger of left hand firmly across three or more strings at any given fret and at the same time leaving the remaining fingers free to stop the strings at the frets indicated. When the first finger is used for the barre chord the thumb should be allowed to come directly under the neck apposite the finger in order to secure a firm hold to the chord.

The following are some of the Barré chords illustrated and explained.

Note: The position which a chord is in is determined by the number of the fret which the first or index finger falls upon.

EXAMPLE. N°1. 2d P. Barre. N°2. 4th P. Barre. N°3. 5th P. Barre. N°4. 7th P. Barre. N°5. 12th P. Barre. N°6.

Chord N° 1. Not a barré chord, by reason of the nut forming a barre of the strings.

N° 2. 2d position Barre. 1st finger across at 2d fret, 3d finger on 1st and 2d strings at 3d fret.

N° 3. Barre at 4th fret and 3d finger across 1st 2d and 3d string at 5th fret.

N° 4. Barre 3 strings at 5th fret and place little finger on 1st string at 7th fret.

N° 5. Barre at 7th fret and place 3d finger on 2d string at 8th fret and little finger on 1st string at 9th fret.

N° 6. Barre three strings at 12th fret and place 2d finger on 2d string at 13th fret and 3d finger on 1st string at 14th fret.

EXERCISES IN TIME.

The above (N? 5) should be first practiced in slow time and then faster as the pupil progresses in execution. In playing in faster time beat the time in stead of counting. Beat with the foot — down, up — down up — or two down and two up in each measure.

Beat time in N? 6, same as N? 5.

EXERCISES IN TIME.

In counting the time to an exercise like the above it is best to count it as $\frac{4}{4}$ so as to make 4 counts or 2 down and 2 up beats in each measure. The same manner of beating time should be used in the following.

In $\frac{2}{4}$ time the accent falls upon the first count. In $\frac{4}{8}$ the same as $\frac{4}{4}$ or common.

First practice the above rather slow counting as $\frac{4}{8}$ time, then practice in polka time counting 1, 2, in each measure — or beating 1 down, and 1 up beat.

EXERCISES IN TIME.

In $\frac{3}{4}$ time the accent always falls upon the first count.

$\frac{6}{8}$ or compound common time is used for Marches, quicksteps, Irish Jigs etc. In beating the time the foot should go down on the first and fourth count the accent falling upon the first and fourth counts.

In $\frac{6}{8}$ time the value of the notes in each measure is the same as in $\frac{3}{4}$ time but the accent as you may perceive is entirely different.

THE SCALES AND CHORDS.

Key of C major, no signature.

A minor Relative to C major.

It will be seen that the Minor scale is not the same ascending and descending. This plan of scale is called the Melodic Minor.

In the Melodic Minor scales the smaller intervals or semitones are from the 2d to 3d note and 7th to 8th note in ascending and from the 6th to 5th and 3d to 2d in descending.

In all the scales in this work the smaller intervals or semitones are denoted by a brace thus "Brace."(............)

Chords in C major.   **A minor.**

Key of G major, with 1 sharp.

Key of E minor.

Chords Key of G major.   **E minor.**

Scale of D major with 2 sharps

B minor.

Chords D major.   **B minor.**

Scale of A major. 3 sharps.

F♯ minor.

Chords A major.   **F♯ minor.**

TONIC CHORDS OF THE 24 KEYS.

As there are twelve semitones in the octave there are consequently twelve keys and as each has its relative minor, we have 24 different key as are shown by the scales etc. preceding.

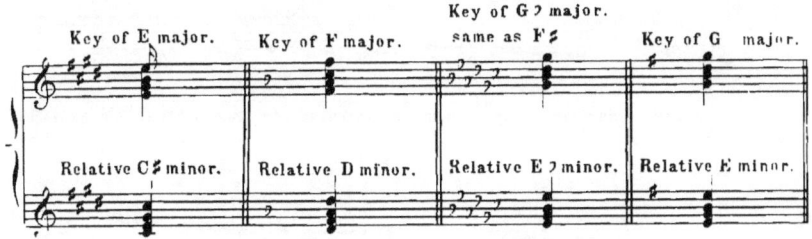

The foregoing are the "tonic" common chords of all of the 24 Major and Minor Keys. The G♭ major may be written as F♯ major and in that case the relative key must be noted as D♯ minor instead of E♭. The Key of D♭ major may also be noted as C♯ major and its relative as A♯ minor. The foregoing chords are not written to be fingered upon the Banjo but merely in their regular order of notation,— of 1st 3d 5th and 8th

EXERCISES.
For Rapid shifting of positions.

Practice the foregoing slowly at first and increase the time until it can be executed rapidly and with ease.

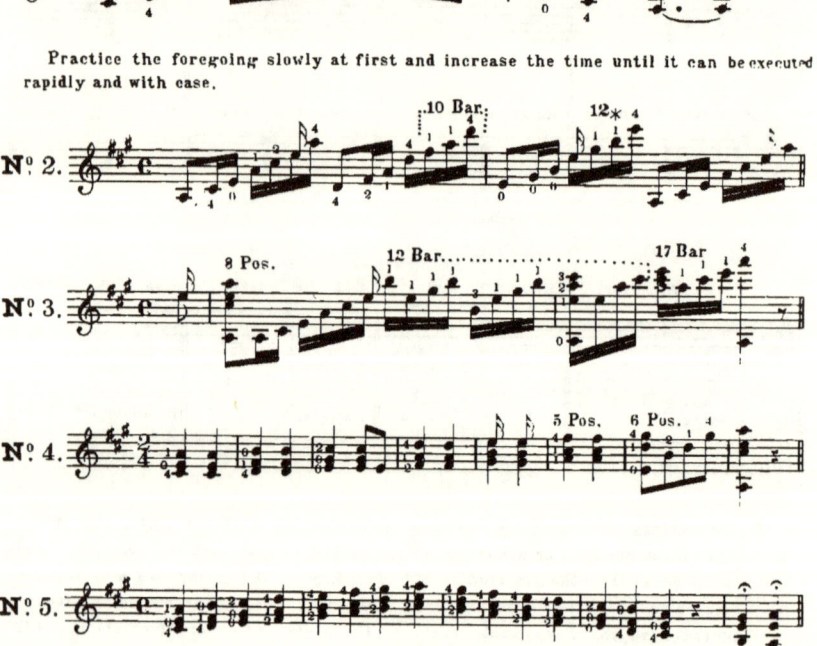

EXERCISES IN WALTZ MOVEMENT.

Pick distinctly, using 3 fingers.

EXERCISES IN MODULATION AND EXPRESSION.

Practice the above exactly as written paying strict attention to the signs.

Both of the above exercises modulate into the dominant key.

This exercise should be practiced with chords as written and also in arpeggio style.

EXERCISES IN THE TREMOLO MOVEMENT.
(See "Observations," page 10.)

The tremolo or trill is made with the first finger of R. H. and no thimble is required. Practice stems turned up on continuous trill. The notes with stems turned down are played with the thumb as an accompaniment to the Tremolo.

Particular attention should be paid to the swells, practicing; the principal effects consisting in the expression from soft to loud and from loud to soft.

THE GRADUATION OF SOUND.
(See "Observations," page 31.)

In playing the tremolo movemet the signs must be fully observed in order to give expression to the music.

It is well to practice the following exercise as written. Much practice is necessary to produce the proper effects.

TREMOLO.
Count 1, 2, 3, 4, to each measure.

Begin the note very soft and increase to loud then reduce to soft again. Play slow:

Count 1, 2, 3, 4, in each measure.

The above differs from the first in as much as the accent or marks of expression are different. Here the first note must begin soft and gradually swell to loud. The next note begins loud and is gradually softened etc.

DRUM CHORDS.
(See page 30 of Observations.)

In playing, "picking," or guitar style, the Drum chords are often introduced into March movements etc. with very fine effect. Drum chords are indicated by the word drum placed over the chord or by the letter D or some suitable sign. The chord so marked is to be struck with the ball of the Thumb and then "rolled," by first closing the hand and rapidly opening the same, (one finger after another beginning with the little finger, and thus making a "roll" over the strings with the back of the nails. This movement will require considerable practice to acquire.

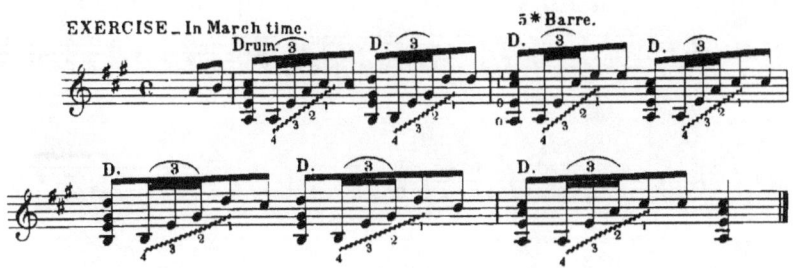

ARPEGGIO OR HARP CHORDS.

In Banjo music we frequently find chords written with a waved line, as in the following examples.

Chords so noted are to be played one note after the other, from the lowest to the highest note, in rapid succession. It is best to pick with the thumb and three fingers. In slow and expressive music this effect is very marked.

EXERCISES WITH BANJO IN "BASS TUNED TO B" STYLE.

It is often necessary in order to obtain certain effects not otherwise readily obtained, to tune the 4th string of the instrument a tone higher in pitch than usual, allowing the other strings to remain as usual.

Pieces to be played with "Bass tuned to B", are so marked on each particular piece. The notes on the Bass string, in that case are of course read differently than when the Bass open is noted as A.

EXERCISES.

THE VIBRATION SLUR AND "SNAP" PASSAGES.

The following melody illustrates the slur in Banjo playing, and the pupil should practice just as written, taking care to make all the notes clearly. Commence by placing the first finger on D♯ and pick the note as written, then instead of picking the next note, E, bring the 2d finger of the left hand down upon the string with as much force as possible. This will cause the note to be made by the vibration of the string and with the peculiar effect of being slurred into the first note. All slurs where the following slurred note is higher than the foregoing note are made in this manner. The second part of the melody illustrates the "snap" slur. This is done where the following slurred note is lower instead of higher. The first note is picked as usual and the next note is made by pulling the string in a dexterous manner with the finger of the left hand which was used to stop the foregoing note. The "snap" is used mainly to facilitate rapid execution, but should be practiced slowly at first.

(See "Observations on the Banjo", page 5.)

Each note must be observed and executed with care and exactness. In music in general the slur indicates that the notes are to be played in a connected manner, termed Legato, but in Violin playing there is a slurred Staccato movement in which the notes are made in one movement of the bow and yet in a short detached manner, which is the most brilliant and effective movement in solo playing. The slurred and snapped passages in Banjo playing may be compared to this Staccato movement. Legato means slow and connected. Staccato means disconnected or detached: It also means distinct. All brilliant execution upon the Banjo is Staccato. The following movement is a sort of combination of the slur and snap movement and requires considerable practice of the left hand, with which it is soley executed.

EXAMPLE 1st.

The first note, only, is picked or struck with the Thumb. The balance of the passage is executed entirely with the 2d finger of left hand a sort of staccato trill. It should be practiced carefully in moderate time and the movement in creased in rapidity as the pupil acquires practice. Such a passage as this is fing. ered in a similar method upon the guitar and in one movement of the Bow upon a Violin.

This method of Trilling is entirely different from the Tremolo movement. which is done with the right hand _ the first finger generally being used.

The following should be practiced in the same manner as the foregoing _

EXAMPLE 2d.

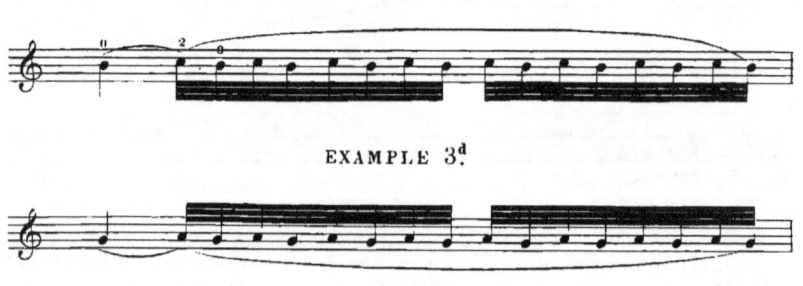

EXAMPLE 3d.

EXAMPLE 4th.

THE HARMONIC TONES.
(See article on the "Harmonic Tones" in back.)

Upon Stringed instruments like the Banjo, Guitar, Violin etc. beautiful effects, called Harmonic notes, may be produced. The Harmonic notes are produced by gently laying a finger of the left-hand on the strings at the proper frets, without pressing the string on the fingerboard. The most perfect Harmonic notes are made at the 5th 12th and 7th frets. Harmonics of all the notes may be made by stoping the string as usual with the left hand fingers and picking the string with the second finger of Right hand, whilst the tip of the first finger of Right hand at the same time touches the string at the desired fret to produce the Harmonic. The harmonic notes do not follow the same law in Acoustics which applies to the ordinary tones. In the harmonics, the string subdivides itself into sections, and their tone corresponds with the quantity of each section in proportion to the length of the string, Thus we find that the harmonic notes produced at the 24th fret will be precisely the same as if produced at the 5th fret. (The 5th fret representing one quarter of the string and the 24th fret the same.) The Harmonic notes produced by touching the strings at the 12th fret sound an octave above the open strings. At the 7th fret a fifth above, and at the 5th fret a double Octave above. When the abbreviation Har. is placed over notes it indicates the Harmonic tones are to be produced.

EXAMPLE.

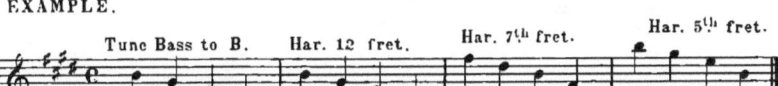

The Harmonics produced sound an Octave above the written notes. If we stop the strings firmly at the 5th fret in the usual manner we produce notes a fourth higher than the open strings _ but if we produce the Harmonics at same fret the sounds produced are 2 octaves above the open strings _ as previously explained.

EMBELLISHMENTS AND GRACE NOTES, CADENZAS Etc.
(See "Observations," page 34.)

Small notes called grace notes or Appoggiatura are often introduced into music by way of embellishment etc. The appoggiatura are of two kinds, long and short.

The long appoggiatura is written in a note of the same or half the value of the note which follows it. It then borrows half the time from the note which follows it.

EXAMPLES.

...written...................... ...played......................

The Short appoggiatura is written differently from the long. It has no fixed value; but is played quite short and borrows only a little of the time of the following note.

Examples of Short grace notes or appoggiatura.

The short grace note is also indicated by a dash across the hook of the note_as follows.

When Grace notes are written as either of the two following examples, the time of the small notes is borrowed from the following notes, and very little time must be allowed for the grace notes which are introduced into the piece by way of embellishment only and not absolutely necessary to the melody. A Cadenze signifies a pause or suspension at the end of an air, which enables the performer to introduce an extempore close. It also signifies an embellishment generally written in small grace notes at the close of a piece.

EXERCISE IN C MAJOR AND A MINOR.

Practice the above in moderate time, taking care to make all the notes distinctly.

EXERCISE IN G MAJOR AND E MINOR.

Practice first strain in Jig Time 4 take care to make all the notes clearly and distinctly. The last strain should be played with expression.

EXERCISE IN D MAJOR AND B MINOR.

Practice in Waltz time, making all the chords distinctly.

EXERCISE IN F MAJOR AND D MINOR.

EXERCISE IN B♭ MAJOR AND G MINOR.

This exercise should be practiced slow and with expression.

EXERCISE IN E♭ MAJOR AND C MINOR.

In practicing the foregoing remember that B. E and A are made flat. In this key the 2d string open would be read as A♭ instead of G♯.

EXERCISES IN STROKE OR THIMBLE PLAYING.

(See "Observations," page 15.)

N.º 1.

In above exercise all the notes except those with double stem are struck down with first finger (thimble) the double stem notes are struck with the thumb.

N.º 2.

ROCK SUSANA.
Weston.

Nº 3. Tune Bass to B.

FREDERICH'S GRAND MARCH.
Nº 4.

DEVIL'S MARCH.
Nº 5.

The two above exercises Nº 4 and 5 are plain stroke with thimble. Thumb not used.

BOCCACCIO MARCH.
Nº 6.

In above exercise slide the thimble over the first chord. The last measure contains a passage which should be played by rolling the thimble over the strings similiar to the first chord. The following exercises are intended for practicing the "Roll" which is much used in march playing with thimble.

Any March written for Banjo which is played stroke style with the thimble may have "drum effects" or "rolls" introduced at the option or taste of the performer. It is not at all necessary to write the "rolls" in the arrangement and indeed it is difficult to do so without making the music appear much more difficult than it really is. Nor do I think there is any advantage in noting the "rolls" in the music as they are in a great manner optional with performer and some performers introduce them with good effect where other players would do better to omit them Some movements may be played with good effect with two roll movements in each measure and again may be made to sound very well with but half the number. In any piece of music where chords are introduced they may be omitted if found too difficult for the performer_ by playing only the uppermost note of the chord which nearly always carries the melody.

MARCH MOVEMENT.

Suppose, for instance, you desire to execute each of the foregoing chords as a "roll" in that case they would be expressed as though written in the following manner.

Or if movement is found too difficult for the performer the rolls may be executed as shown in the following example.

By practicing the illustrations given here the pupil will readily acquire the execution of the roll and learn to introduce the same at pleasure in any of his favorite marches. It is best, however, to practice the March first without the rolls and introduce them after the performer has become quite familiar with the Melody and requisite chords. Many performers introduce the rolls into their marches without regard to proper chords, but in a large room or hall the discord, (which would be bad if heard near the performer,) is not perceived, owing to the law of acoustics that Sound travels further than noise. The discordant effects die away and the harmonious sounds are heard only. It is better however to learn to express the proper chords if you would be classed as an artist.

CHORDS.

There are only twelve original chords of each kind, but they can be almost infinitely varied. The following are the Harmonic names of the chords of the different degrees of the Major and minor scales.

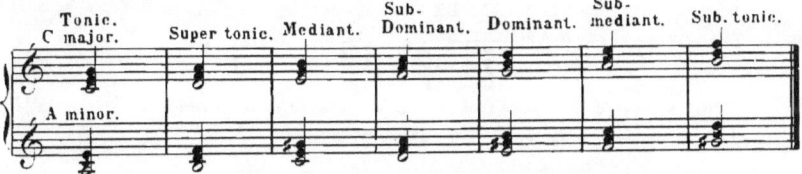

The above may be transposed into any key and the positions of the notes altered to suit the Banjo fingering.

The Dominant key of any scale is always the fifth letter in the scale, Many pieces of music modulate into the dominant of their key and often into the sub dominant.

MODULATION.

Many compositions are not confined to any one key or scale but are often partly in one key and partly in another — but returning to their original key before closing. Passing from one key into another in a graceful and pleasing manner is called Modulation. For instance, we have a composition beginning in the key of E, and the next strain changing to the key of A. (or sub dominant key) A very simple manner of modulating in this instance is as per following example.

Supposing the last chord before changing key to be E we then make the dominant seventh chord of the key A, which brings us immediately into that key.

EXAMPLE.

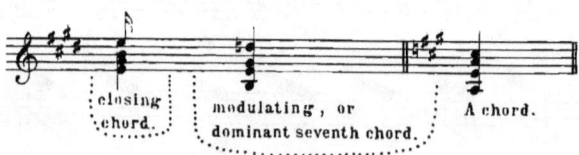

closing chord.   modulating, or dominant seventh chord.   A chord.

This is the most simple way of modulating known. The dominant seventh chord is used before passing into the key to which it belongs and is all that is required in changing when the keys are nearly related to each other; but when the keys are not closely related to each other more complicated modulations are often necessary.

Suppose we wish to change from the key of A into the key of D. We make the dominant seventh chord belonging to the new key before making the tonic chord of that key.

See following
EXAMPLE.

Or suppose we desire to change from A to E we proceed in the same way.

EXAMPLE.

The keys of A D and E major are closely related and hence the modulations from one to the other are very simple.

EXPLANATION OF THE DOMINANT AND DOMINANT SEVENTH CHORDS.

The dominant note of any scale is always the fifth letter in that scale. Hence the dominant chord of the key is formed by adding to this note its third fifth and eighth. This is then called the dominant chord. If the seventh is added instead of the eighth the chord is then called the dominant seventh.

Take for, instance, the key of C.

The following is its dominant seventh chord:

Dominant seventh chord to Key of C.

Now if we were playing in the key of G, with F♯ and desired to run into the key of C, we would form this chord, and of course place a natural (♮) before the F.

THE DIMINISHED SEVENTH.

A diminished seventh is formed by sharping the root of the chord of seventh.

Changing the position of the notes in a chord does not alter the harmony of the chord. It is frequently necessary to change the notes around in order to make the chord at all upon the Banjo: (and in fact the same may be said of the guitar or any other string instrument upon which harmony is played)

In transposing chords from the Piano copy it is necessary to often alter the position of notes to make fingering possible. See following

EXAMPLES.

Chords in Regular order.

Chords adapted to Banjo. (with proper fingering)

TRANSPOSITION

The following is a simple melody first written in the key of C Major and then transposed into the six other letters of the diatonic scale of C Major, making the same melody in seven keys.

The Student should write the Tonic, Subdominant and Dominant chords of the fore-going melody in each of the seven keys.

DARKIES PASTIME (Minor Jig)

The time in above Jig may be tapped with the foot, 4 taps to each measure — which is the method generally adopted in playing Jigs.

HOME SWEET HOME.
Moderato. with Expression.

The foregoing melody should be played slowly and care taken to bring out the harmony and expression. Use the three fingers in picking. The Chords with waved lines are "harp chords" should be played arpeggio style or disconnected.

MISCELLANEOUS EXERCISES.

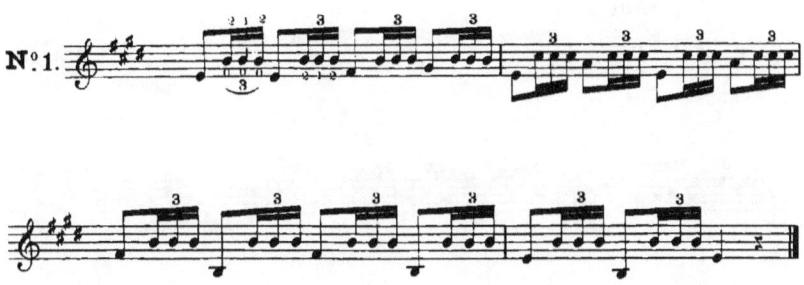

In the foregoing exercise the triplets should be executed by picking with 2 fingers instead of with 1 finger. This greatly facilitates rapid execution and is some times called rolling.

EXTRACT FROM W. A. HUNTLEY'S "ROCKY POINT SCHOTTISCHE."
(Copyrighted 1883 by S S Stewart.)

HORNPIPE.

Nº 3.

Extract from the "SEEK NO FURTHER" MARCH. (Copyrighted 1883 by S.S.Stewart.)

Nº 4.

In the foregoing the time should be strongly marked by accenting each of the notes so marked. The accented notes should be struck down with the Thumb of R. H. with considerable force.

HORNPIPE.

Nº 5.

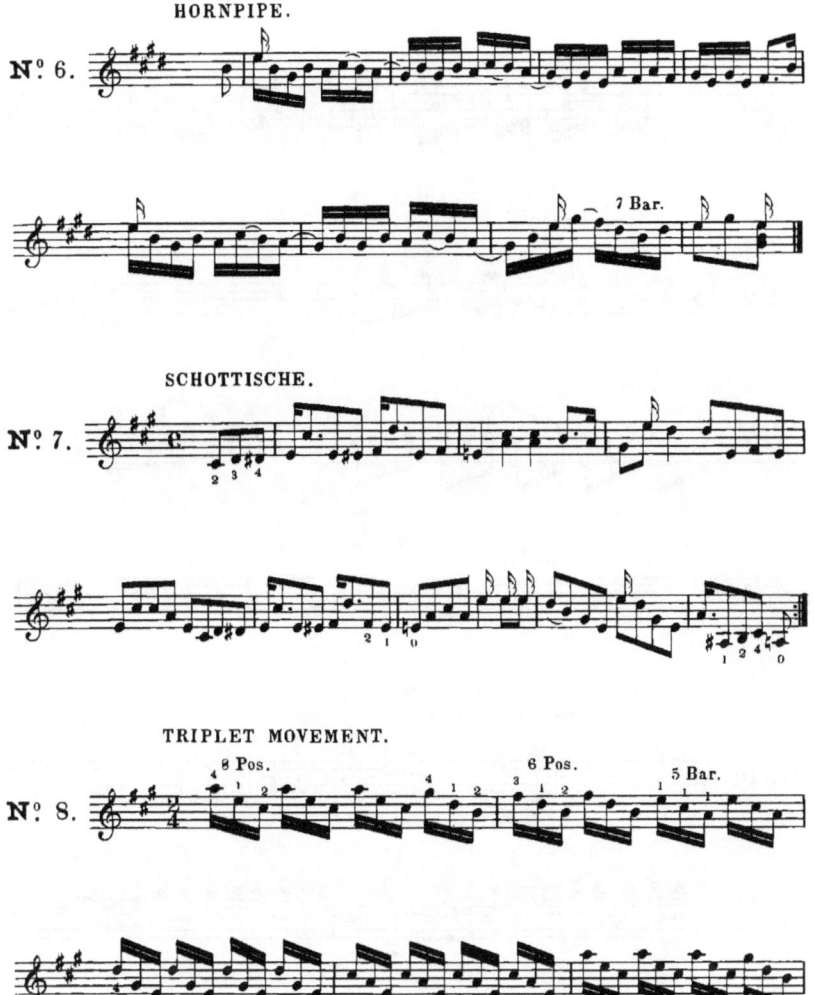

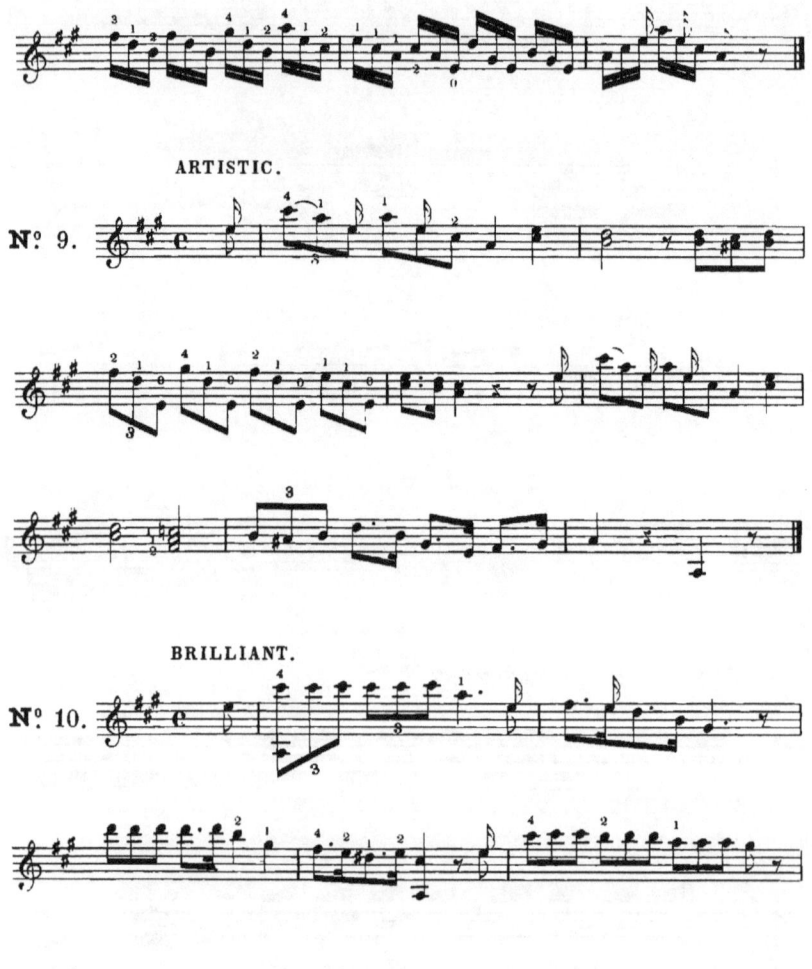

ACCOMPANIMENTS FOR SONGS

"SWANEE RIVER." *(This song with piano accomp't. published by Oliver Ditson Co., Boston, Mass. Price 30 cts.)*

The following is same accompaniment differently arranged.

BLUE BELLS OF SCOTLAND.

The pupil should transpose Nº 5 into the key of E and practice in each of the keys, E and A.

The following (Nº 6) is the second strain of the foregoing arranged with a different harmony.

THE OLD KENTUCKY HOME

No. 7.

This song with Piano accompt. published by
Oliver Ditson Co, Boston, Mass. Price 40 cts.

NELLY GRAY

No. 8.

EMBELLISHMENTS AND CADENZA EXERCISES.

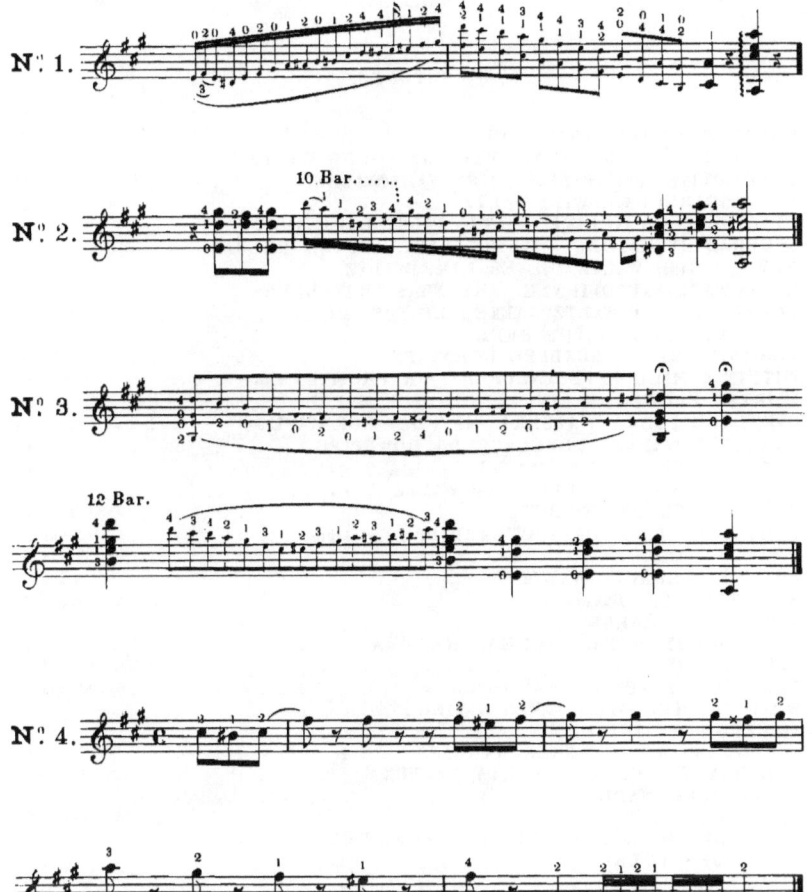

THE COMPLETE AMERICAN BANJO SCHOOL.

PART II.

CONTENTS.

WALTZ FOR PUPIL AND TEACHER	51
ON YONDER ROCK. WINE, WIFE AND SONG WALTZ	52
LOCOMOTIVE HORNPIPE. FAIRY VARSOVIENNE	53
LA ZINGARELLA. SWISS WALTZ	54
BEETHOVEN'S FAVORITE WALTZ. FIRST LOVE REDOWA	55
SCHERZO BY HAYDN. MANDOLINATA. SCOTCH MELODY	56
NEW SPANISH WALTZ. SILVER LAKE WALTZ	57
HOLLOWAY'S VARSOVIENNE. ARKANSAS TRAVELLER	58
EGYPTIAN HARP WALTZ. VEXED EDITOR'S REEL	59
MORTON'S REEL. BATH'S REEL	60
VIRGINIA REEL. DUXBURG HORNPIPE	61
WITHIN A MILE OF EDINBURGH. AIR FROM ZAMPA	62
FAIREST FLOWER WALTZ. OLD STYLE WALTZ	63
OVERLAND POLKA MAZURKA. MAY DAY HORNPIPE	64
LANDLER'S WALTZ. DOUBLE CLOG HORNPIPE	65
APPROACH OF SPRING WALTZES	66
WITCHE'S DANCE. LAUTERBACH WALTZ	67
VARSOVIENNE BY STRAUSS	68
THE BLUE BELLS OF SCOTLAND with Variations	69 and 70
AMAZON MARCH	71 and 72
CHARMING BEAUTY WALTZES	73 and 74
NORMA MARCH (Duet)	75, 76 and 77
MERRY WAR MARCH	78
SNOW SCHOTTISCHE. GERMAN REDOWA	79
SECRET LOVE	80 and 81
CARNIVAL OF VENICE with Variations	82, 83 and 84
WHAT ARE THE WILD WAVES SAYING	85
AIR FROM MASANIELLO	85
SOUNDS FROM THE NORTH WALTZES	86
ONE HEART ONE SOUL POLKA MAZURKA	87 and 88
ANGEL'S SERENADE	89
SPANISH FANDANGO	89 and 90
ADJUTANTS QUICKSTEP. FIREFLY HORNPIPE	91
SYLPHIDEN POLKA	92
TIVOLI GALOP	93
COLLOSEUM HORNPIPE	94
ELECTRIC SPARK'S WALTZES	95
REITER GALOP	96
EN PLEINE CHASSE GALOP	97
SILESIA POLKA	98
DIE FRÖHLICHE SPINNERIN POLKA	99

Copyright 1883 by S. S. Stewart.

THE COMPLETE AMERICAN BANJO SCHOOL.
PART II.

WALTZ FOR PUPIL AND TEACHER.
S. S. Stewart.

Copyright 1883 by S. S. Stewart.

ON YONDER ROCK RECLINING.
from FRA DIAVOLO.

WINE, WIFE AND SONG WALTZ.

STRAUSS.

LOCOMOTIVE CLOG HORNPIPE.

FAIRY VARSOVIENNE.

LA ZINGARELLA.

THE SWISS WALTZ.

BEETHOVEN'S FAVORITE WALTZ.

FIRST LOVE REDOWA.

SCHERZO, FROM HAYDN'S SYMPHONY.

MANDOLINATA.

SCOTCH MELODY.

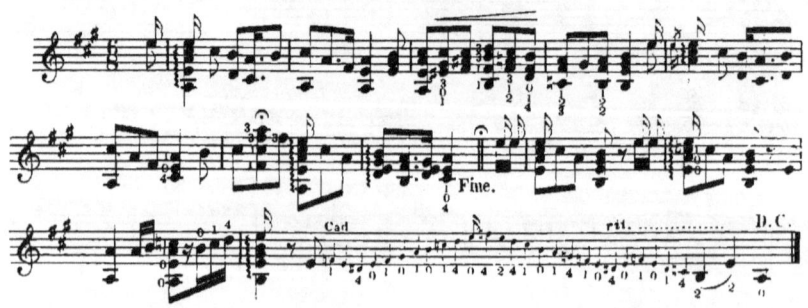

NEW SPANISH WALTZ.

SILVER LAKE WALTZ.

HOLLOWAY'S VARSOVIENNE.

ARKANSAS TRAVELER.

EGYPTIAN HARP WALTZ.

THE VEXED EDITOR'S REEL.

MORTON'S REEL.

CHARLE'S BATH'S REEL.

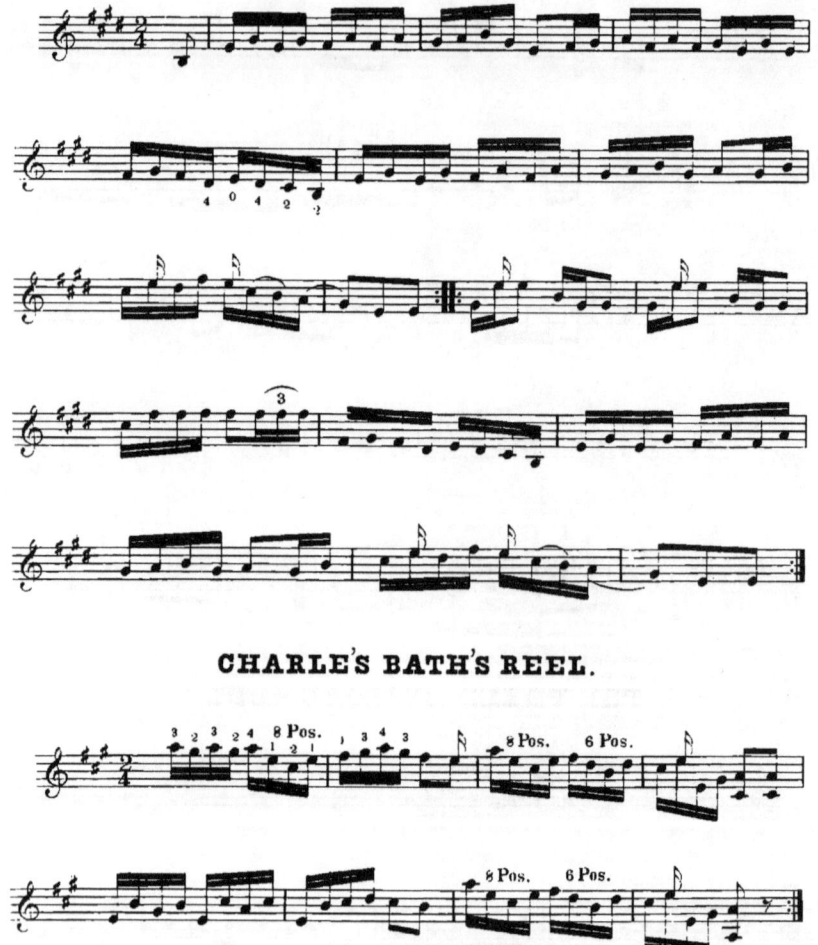

THE VIRGINIA REEL.

DUXBURY HORNPIPE.

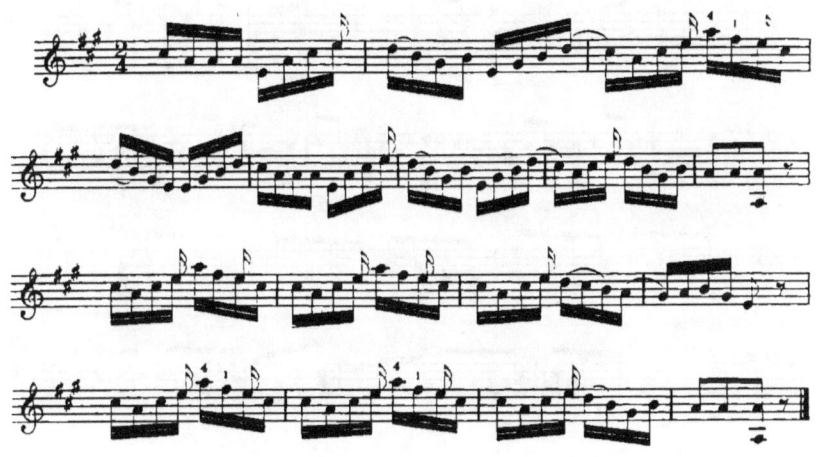

WITHIN A MILE OF EDINBURGH.

AIR FROM ZAMPA.

FAIREST FLOWER WALTZ.

OLD STYLE WALTZ.

OVERLAND POLKA MAZURKA

MAY DAY HORNPIPE.

LANDLER'S WALTZ.

DOUBLE CLOG HORNPIPE.

APPROACH OF SPRING WALTZES.

Fr. Zikoff.

WITCHES DANCE.

Introduction. Paganini.

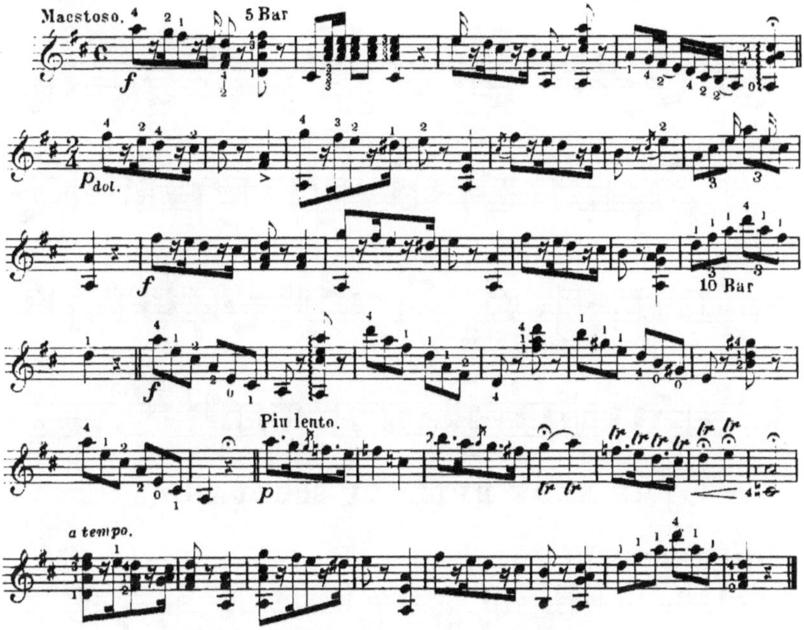

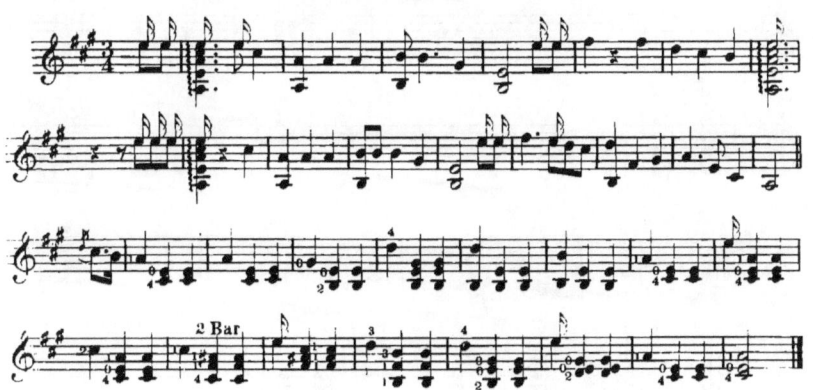

THE LAUTERBACH WALTZ.

VARSOVIENNE BY STRAUSS.

THE BLUE BELLS OF SCOTLAND.

S. S. Stewart.

BLUE BELLS OF SCOTLAND.

VAR. I.

BLUE BELLS OF SCOTLAND—Concluded.

VAR. II.

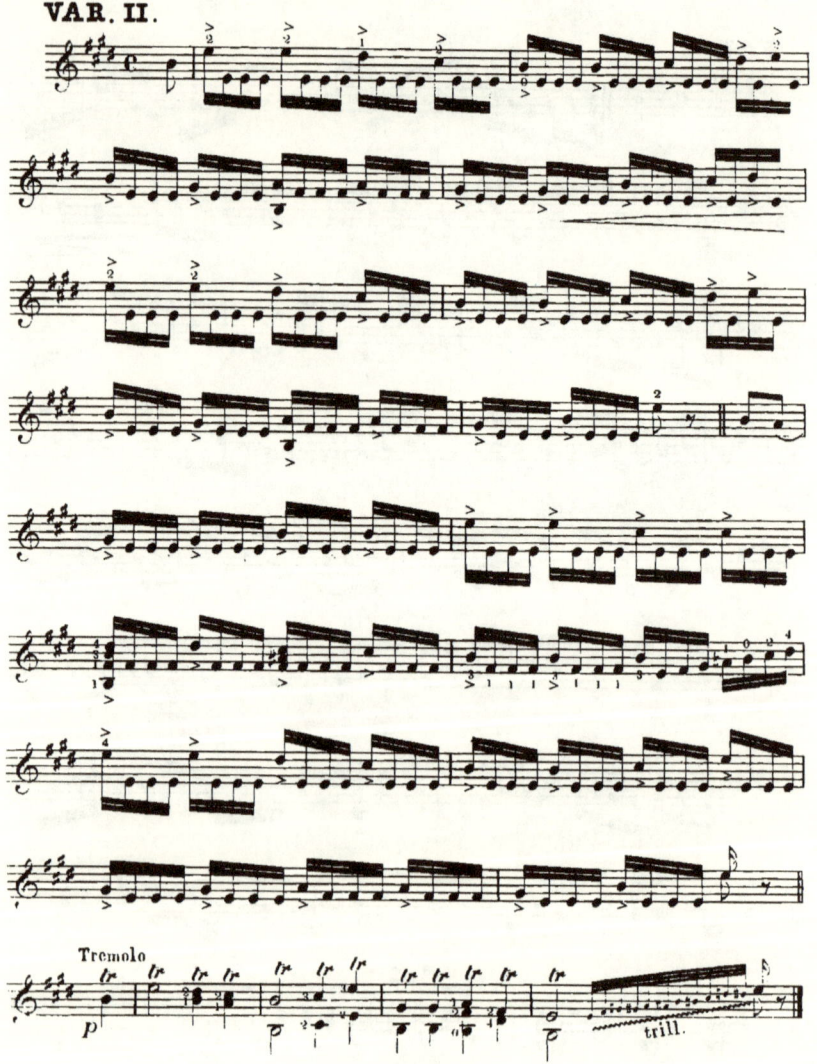

THE AMAZON MARCH.

G. Michaelis.

THE AMAZON MARCH—Concluded.

D. C. Mch. to Fine.

THE CHARMING BEAUTY WALTZES

Fr. Zikoff.

THE NORMA MARCH

THE NORMA MARCH—Concluded.

THE NORMA MARCH Concluded.

THE MERRY WAR MARCH.

arranged for the Banjo. Strauss.

SNOW SCHOTTISCHE.

GERMAN REDOWA.

//2

THE CARNIVAL OF VENICE with VARIATIONS.

Stewart.

WHAT ARE THE WILD WAVES SAYING.

AIR FROM MASANIELLO.

SOUNDS FROM THE NORTH WALTZES.

Zikoff.

ONE HEART ONE SOUL.

POLKA MAZURKA   J. STRAUSS.

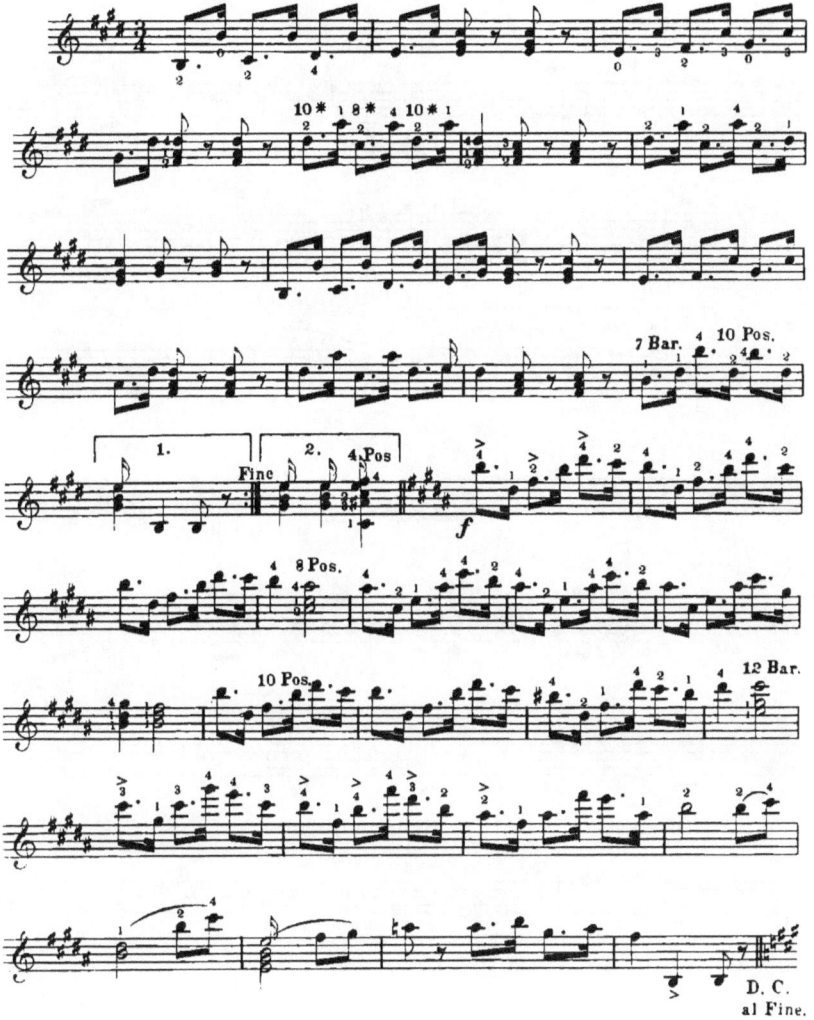

ANGEL'S SERENADE.

G. Braga.

To be played Tremolo.
Andante con motto.

SPANISH FANDANGO.

Introduction.
Andante, with Expression.

Tune Bass to B.

FANDANGO.

The Fandango should be played in Waltz time and with expression. The Variations possible to construct from this melody are boundless.

ADJUTANTS QUICKSTEP.

FIREFLY HORNPIPE.

SYLPHIDEN POLKA

Zikoff.

TIVOLI GALOP.

Zikoff.

ELECTRIC SPARK'S WALTZES.

Zikoff.

REITER GALOP.

Zikoff.

EN PLEINE CHASSE GALOP.

Zikoff.

SILESIA POLKA.

Zikoff.

DIE FRÖHLICHE SPINNERIN POLKA.

Zikoff.

The Complete American Banjo School

Contents of Supplements, and additions to the Work, up to January, 1893

CHORDS, MAJOR AND MINOR, in the key of A Major. . . . .

CHORD EXERCISE in A Major. . . . .

MODULATIONS IN FOURTHS, through all keys. . . . .

PRACTICAL INSTRUCTIONS IN THE NATURAL HARMONIES OF THE BANJO.

OBSERVATIONS ON STROKE OR THIMBLE PLAYING.

"THE BANJO PHILOSOPHICALLY." (Nine Pages). . . .

AN EXPOSITION OF HARMONIC TONES. . . . .

HOW TO PUT A HEAD ON A BANJO. (Illustrated). . . .

REMARKS ON THE BANJO FINGER-BOARD, THE CHROMATIC SCALE, . .

. . . . . TUNING, FRETTING, etc. (Illustrated). . . . . . .

POSITION OF HOLDING THE BANJO. . . . .

"OBSERVATIONS ON THE BANJO AND BANJO PLAYING," . . . .

An illustrated article of thirty-five pages, treating upon the following: Various methods of fingering. Musical examples of the same. Left hand positions, with illustrations from photographs. The "Tremolo" movement, illustrated. Musical examples in tremolo playing. The stroke tremolo. Stroke playing, illustrated. The handling of the pegs. The Banjo bridge. The Banjo strings. The head, the rim, the neck. Remarks on Banjo heads. To prevent the head becoming too dry. The bridge in position. Available keys. Fingering the fifth string. The minor scales explained. Notation and pitch. Concert pitch. Reading in the positions. Drum chords. Musical expression. Exercise in "Double Stops." Embellishments. Grace notes. The six string Banjo. Concluding remarks.

ADVANCED EXERCISES FOR THE BANJO. (Three pages). . . . .

The Banjo Philosophically.

Its Construction, Its Capabilities, Its Evolution, Its place as a Musical Instrument. Its possibilities, and Its Future.

Copyright, 1886, by S. S. Stewart.

A LECTURE,
By S. S. STEWART.

I have selected as my subject THE PHILOSOPHICAL PRINCIPLES OF THE BANJO AND BANJO PLAYING. More properly speaking, I should say, THE PHILOSOPHICAL BASIS ON WHICH THE BANJO IS CONSTRUCTED, AND THE PHILOSOPHY OF BANJO PLAYING.

I have here several banjos and parts which it is my purpose to introduce, and which I shall use as objects of illustration during the course of my lecture.

I ask your attention, for a short time, to my remarks, and I will endeavor to bring before you, in as unpretentious manner as possible, the different classes and grades of banjos, and notice briefly the various changes which have taken place in the instrument during the past thirty years, during its process of evolution to its present state of progression.

The banjo is, as you all know, an instrument of the stringed class, and may be associated with the guitar, lute, mandolin, bandore, etc.

I believe, and it is so stated by other authorities, that the banjo got its name from the *bandore*, and that it is not of negro origin as has been claimed.

The *bandore* some of you have heard played, when you listened to the Original Spanish Students.

It is of ancient origin and the name banjo is thought to have been corrupted therefrom.

There is no such instrument as a *bandoline*, so far as my knowledge extends, although I have heard that name mentioned in connection with banjos.

Bandoline, as I understand it, is a hair oil or pomade, and can have no signification here.

The name *Banjourine* has been given to a somewhat modern style of banjo of my own manufacture, and of which I shall have something to say presently.

I mentioned some time ago in a small publication relating to the banjo, that an Egyptian Lyre of the Ancient Egyptians had been seen by a certain writer, which was in every respect a modern banjo. I believe that the hoop or rim of this lyre was oblong or oval, not circular, like ours—hence it was not a "modern banjo."

However, it is not my purpose to delve into by-gone ages, searching after fragments of the past—at least at this time; nor is it my purpose to dwell upon the origin and ancestry of the present banjo, nor to occupy any more of your time by dwelling upon or discussing as to where, why, when and how the banjo got its name.

We all admit that it has a name and that its name is banjo—b-a-n-j-o or b-a-n-j-e-a-u, but not b-a-n-r. This is sufficient.

The instrument, as it stands, is composed of a circular frame or rim, over which a membraneous substance, called the head, is stretched. This head being elastic acts as a sound-board, as does also, in a manner, the wood or other material in the rim or circular frame.

The instrument, like the guitar and other instruments of its class, has a neck; from the extreme end of which strings are stretched, extending over the head, across the circular frame.

A small piece of wood is fashioned into a "bridge," upon which the strings rest, and by which their vibration is conducted to the head. Without this small appendage, the bridge, the instrument would be worthless.

The banjo differs in the tone produced, as well as in its shape and general appearance, from the guitar and other instruments of the same class.

The strings vibrate, and are treated in a similar manner to the strings upon a guitar, but the philosophy and scientific principles of the construction of the instrument are different.

In the banjo the head combines its vibration or pulsations with the vibrations of the strings, and the rim acts in unison with the head as a peculiar kind of sound-board. But of this I shall have more to say later on.

THE EARLY BANJO.

Should any of you open *Moore's Encyclopedia of Music* at page 90, and there read its description of a banjo, you would possibly be led to believe that the banjo was not much of a musical instrument. And you would infer rightly; for at the time the *Encyclopedia* was published, in the year 1854, I believe, the banjo was considered, as some have it, purely an instrument of accompaniment. In those days no one supposed that the banjo would ever become a recognized and favorite musical instrument, or that it could ever possibly become a favorite with the ladies.

Time works great changes, and yet I have no doubt that many there are who still have no other conception of the banjo than as described in Moore's and other Encyclopedias.

About the first player upon the banjo I have heard spoken of was Joe Sweeney, of Virginia. Before his day the instrument is said to have been a "three-string gourd," and played by one Picayune Butler, of whom many of you have heard. There was a great old-time "banjo song," said to have been sung by him, called "*Picayune Butler's Come to Town.*"

But as Picayune Butler's Three String Gourd bears as little relation to the present banjo as the ancient *Viol* does, or did, to our present *Violin*, the king of musical instruments, I deem it worthy of but brief mention at present.

Sweeney, aforesaid, is said to have added the third and fifth strings to the "three string gourd" and made it, what was at that time called a banjo.

The banjo at that time had no hoop and system of screw hooks to tighten the head. The head or skin was usually fastened to the rim with tacks and cement.

The head, after being wet, was stretched over the circular rim, which was usually of ash wood, and then fastened and allowed to dry.

When the head dried it of course contracted and became firm and tight. We have still in use almost the identical system for putting heads on tambourines, but the old-fashioned "tack head" banjo has gone out of date—burned out, like a taper or tallow dip, which has given place to the lamp, gas jet and electric light.

Following the "tack head" banjo came the screw-head banjo with solid iron band or hoop and iron brackets and screws.

It was no longer necessary to hold the banjo near a stove in order to cause the head to contract and become tight when the weather was damp, as the nuts upon the hooks could be screwed up and the hoop drawn down in a somewhat similar manner as it is done to-day.

But the banjo at best was a very crude instrument. The system, or mechanical part of the same, was very unfinished, and the heads in use were generally made of sheepskin, and were not calculated to stand the strain which those used to-day are put to.

The necks, too, were very crude, and generally had a piece of wood sliced out of the butt-end, adjoining the rim and hoop, as nobody ever thought of playing "Away up There" in those days.

* Then, too, the instrument was strung with thick strings and tuned to a low pitch, and the style of execution was entirely the old "stroke," or original "banjo style." Nobody "picked" the banjo then in what is now termed "guitar style."

They used to make the banjo rims in those days at least three inches in depth, which made them look clumsy and "tubby."

In those days there was a banjo maker in New York by the name of Jacobs. He is spoken of as the first "professional banjo maker," or first maker of "professional banjos."

That means that he did not make fancy banjos for the ladies to decorate with ribbons and hang up in their boudoirs, but he made a good, solid, strong, heavy-built banjo, which was calculated to stand the hard knocks of the minstrel stage.

I have never, so far as I know, seen or played upon one of Jacobs' instruments, but I think if I could produce one of them that you would scarcely recognize in it any resemblance to our favorite "silver-rim" banjo of to-day, now so popular.

Jacobs was evidently an industrious German, and returned to his native land with a small fortune, made by hard work and saved by frugal living.

It may be that he introduced into Germany the patterns from which some factories are still turning out banjos, but I hesitate to charge an honest man with such a crime.

However, Jacobs lived and made his banjos before my time, that is, before I saw the light in this world; and I will refrain, therefore, from raking over the ashes of by-gone days, now buried in oblivion.

From time to time improvements were made in the banjo as it developed in the hands of new performers. Mechanics here and there improved its various parts, and gradually musicians "took hold" of it.

More brackets were added to the rim; some makers narrowed down their rims a little, and also shortened their necks, and then banjos began to appear having polished brass or German silver brackets and hooks instead of iron. A gaudy brass plate was sometimes set into the neck as a part of the finger-board.

Players began to execute music in the guitar style of playing, and the banjo began to receive great attraction in all minstrel shows.

G. Swayne Buckley was one of the first who added the guitar style of *frets* to his banjo, although I believe that he played almost entirely "banjo" or "stroke" style, and therefore his wisdom in using *frets* (raised frets) was doubted by many.

At that time scarcely any performer used frets, raised or otherwise—on a banjo neck.

Indeed there would have been little use for them with most of the "great banjo soloists" of that day, as they never thought of stopping the strings beyond the fifth string peg. The gigantic effort required in making a *barre chord* on the banjo then used was not to be indulged in by any, save those of advanced musical views and good physical development.

I have endeavored to be as brief as possible in my remarks, as the ground already covered is but an introduction to what follows.

I will, therefore, now take up the THE BANJO—the *silver rim banjo*—which I consider the only true banjo, and endeavor to philosophise and analyze the instrument in as few words as possible.

THE "SILVER RIM" BANJO.

Just as there are enormous numbers of trade fiddles, cheap violins, turned out of the great toy shop of the world, Germany, and sold by our music stores throughout the land, so there are factories in this country, where large numbers of cheap banjos are manufactured and supplied to the trade.

The old style "tack-head" banjo is scarcely found in a music store to-day, but it is sometimes to be found at toy stores, where they are disposed of to young ladies, some of whom purchase them for cheap decorating purposes. But the majority of banjos turned out by the "cheap factories" at this time are metal covered rim banjos, with nickel plated mountings and walnut necks. They are made in imitation of the Standard German Silver Rim "Professional" Banjo, and sold to beginners and learners of the instrument. Nearly all of my recent customers have had at least one of these cheap banjos. In fact I prefer that such should be the case, as a person who

... been in the habit of playing upon a poor instrument ... all the more ready to appreciate a good one when he gets it, although it may be that his "musical ear" has been deadened to some extent.

Many of you have heard of the old "Troy Banjo." A few years ago these banjos were in use by many players upon the stage and thought much of. They were made by two makers: The first was Albert Wason, an eccentric genius, who was much liked by many players of his day. Wilson was followed by a maker named William H. Farnham, who followed the style originated by Wilson, without attempting any great improvement. These banjos were generally of 10½, 11 and 11½ inch rim. The necks were bolted fast to the rims, there being no wood or metal bar extending from the neck through the rim as there is ... nearly all banjos of the present day. The absence of this bar caused the neck to constantly work upwards, an l the banjo could not be depended upon to remain in tune.

The rims of these instruments were constructed upon the same principles as those of to-day. A maple wood hoop, covered with sheet German silver, and turned down at each side over a wire ring. But the work was more crude at that period, and the rims, although very strong and solidly made, were not capable of giving the vibration of those produced and used this day in the Stewart Banjo. This is a well attested fact.

The "Clarke Banjo," an improvement on the Wilson and Farnham Banjos, became a general favorite among minstrel and other stage performers.

Clarke's Banjos were made by the late Jas. W. Clarke, who continued to make them until the time of his death, which was caused by consumption, and took place in New York City, on February 27th, 1880. Clarke's Banjos, as I have said, were an improvement on the Wilson or Farnham instrument, as Clarke added the extension bar to the necks, making the instrument more solid in construction, and more sure to remain in tune. But I do not mean to say that Clarke was by any means the inventor of this improvement, or that it was of his own origination, for the majority of wood rim banjos, even before that day, were so made. But every manufacturer of a musical instrument leaves the impress of his individuality in his work, to a certain extent. This is a perfectly philosophical and a well known psychological fact, and governed by a psychological law.

Outside of this, Clarke had his little secrets in regard to his methods of work, just as every skilled workman and specialist has to-day, and as well, many little points which would scarcely be of much service to another maker, for every true genius has his natural and original ways of working.

Clarke's Banjos were noted for their loud and sharp tone, it being a standard among professional banjo players, that if you wanted a "sharp banjo" you must get a Clarke.

There are makers to-day, who, instead of branching out and studying their subject, and endeavoring to get up instruments better than others, which is the only legitimate way in which a demand for their instruments can be created, are content to plod along, copying the Stewart Banjo and the patterns of other makers.

Such makers very seldom amount to anything. No two men have the same individuality, and hence it is silly for one man to copy another. The true banjo maker needs no copy, his model is formed in the mind, and he works out his own ideas. Those makers who possess no ideas of their own had better, far better, seek some other means of gaining a livelihood.

On the other hand, we have manufacturers who are constantly inflicting upon the banjo what they are pleased to designate as "improvements," upon which they have patented.

We have had patent-closed backs, patent hoops, patent hollow rims, patent bell rims, patent keys, patent bracket protectors, patent tail pieces, patent tie attachments, patent arm rests, patent tone ... and a variety of other patents; but none of these have added one jot nor tittle to the musical value of the banjo.

The "silver-rim banjo," as described, has been for years past the standard banjo; THE BANJO among professional players of note, and the number of patent banjos" of any kind in use by noted players, or even skilled amateurs, has always been very small.

There are, and have been, "wooden-rim" banjos in use on the stage at various times by performers, and although the great majority of this class of banjos may be rated as "tubs," yet a really good instrument of wood rim is sometimes to be found.

And yet, in these banjos, there is almost always to be found metal of some kind, combined with the wood. It may be only an iron or brass strip or wire ring, intended merely to strengthen the rim, but it nevertheless has its effect upon the tone of the instrument.

I can, therefore, confidently assert that the standard banjo, with players of eminence and skill, is a banjo with a metal and wood rim used in combination.

The Stewart Banjos, as manufactured by myself at the present time, are simply claimed to be improvements upon the same style of banjo manufactured by others before me.

On my banjos proper I claim no new invention, nor have I any patents connected therewith. (This remark has no reference to the improved *Banjeaurine*.)

But I do claim an improved and more perfected banjo, secured by new processes of manufacture, some of which remain secrets of my own, and which to attempt to protect by letters patent would merely place part of my knowledge in the hands of others. I also claim a skill in the construction of banjos, the result of a *natural musical gift*, together with a somewhat extended experience as a performer upon the instrument, and a student of the science of music, which, together with experimenting and constant observation, has aided me, and added to my adaptability in this, my particular line of business.

Without any egotistical feelings whatever, I am able to point with pride to the letters from our most talented, prominent and eminent players of the banjo; in fact, foremost artists of the day, testifying to the merits of the banjos manufactured by me, and of their many points of superiority over the instruments of other manufacturers.

I do not assert that the banjos I manufacture are perfect; nor do I believe that those of any other maker are perfect; or that anything produced on this earth is or ever has been *perfect*. But whatever assertions regarding my banjos I have made have been certified to and fully indorsed; in fact, more fully than I have ever asked, by players of eminence who have no pecuniary interest whatever in my business or my banjos.

Neither do I assume to know all there is to be learned about banjo making or any other art, science or philosophy. What I may know to-day I may discover, to-morrow, that I do not know. What seems in place to-day may seem out of place to-morrow, and vice versa.

I expect to learn something new every day, and all that can be expected of me to-day is that I shall give you my views and ideas as they exist at the present time.

I have asserted, and can readily demonstrate by letters from leading players, that the banjo of *German silver and wood combined rim* is and has been for a long time *the banjo*—the recognized banjo of the artist banjo player.

This banjo has a perfectly scientific and philosophical basis of construction, in fact is constructed in as philosophically correct a manner as the guitar, man doline, zither or any other stringed instrument. Its body consists of a circular frame, called the rim. This rim, as you will notice, has a bright and attractive appearance. It is composed of the alloy known as German silver on the outside, and maple wood upon the inside. They are, in fact, two separate and distinct rims so united as to act as one.

We attach to this combination, or rim, a system of brackets, which are so made as to admit of hooks with screw threads cut on them passing through them, and a suitable nut being fitted to each of the several screws.

With these hooks or screws, and by the aid of this bright and neatly-finished band or hoop, we are enabled to adjust the important factor called the head. The head is a membrane or membraneous skin, and is, as shown, adjusted and tightly stretched upon or over the rim or circular frame.

When this is completed we have, as you see before you, the body of the instrument almost complete.

Next, we have the neck of walnut, maple, cherry, rose or other suitable wood, which must be accurately fitted and correctly adjusted to the body of the instrument. We call the upper surface of the neck the *finger-board*, for over this surface the strings are stretched, which are vibrated to produce the musical sounds.

Were it not for this neck surface, the finger-board, we should have only five notes or sounds, as produced by the live strings of the banjo.

This is, of course, speaking only for the regular five-string banjo; some banjos being constructed with additional strings.

The musical strings are stretched from the appendage called the *tail-piece*, which, by the way, was often termed *apron* in days gone by ; so termed, I presume, from its large size and close resemblance to the article of female dress designated by that name—over the extreme end of the finger-board, running through notches in this little piece of ivory called the nut, to the pegs, by the turning of which we are enabled to tighten the strings or after their tension, either one way or the other at pleasure.

The bridge—this insignificant little piece of maple—over which the strings pass, rests firmly upon the head in the position you see in this instrument. Without the bridge the banjo would be useless as a musical instrument.

When the strings are set in vibration, which is done with the fingers of the right hand, the vibrations produce motion in the air, which we term *sound waves*. The sound waves being in close proximity to the head are reverberated by it, and the bridge acting as a conductor of sound, also transmits the vibrations to the head, which is elastic, and these double vibrations, so to speak, are transmitted through the air.

Thus the head acts as a sound-board by which the sound waves caused by the vibration of stretched strings are transmitted, and at the same time is itself a sonorous body, having, so to speak, an independent vibration, and thus plays a double part in the construction of the instrument.

The rim, too, plays an all-important part in the vibrating power of the instrument, and is, in fact, the entire foundation upon which the musical quality, quantity and power of the banjo's tone must be built.

The head, as I have shown, is tightly stretched over the rim, and is itself sonorous, the requisite necessary for producing sound of any kind.

Thus the head having a flat, smooth surface, becomes an excellent sound-board, and being circular in shape, is well calculated to transmit sound waves, which are, so to speak, floating circles.

The head thus tightly drawn over the rim acts in unison therewith. It must act in unison with the rim or we will have a poor banjo.

Thus the head and the rim are united, they are parts of one whole; they must unite and become as ONE just as surely as the pine-wood top of the guitar becomes one with the guitar when it is attached thereto by glue.

The vibration of the strings then, it is conceded, is conducted to the head by means of the bridge, and to the rim by means of the head, and the rim must be so constructed as to respond to and mingle its vibrations with those of the head and strings, forming one harmonious whole.

When the head is wet or damp it is slack, and when in that condition the banjo will not produce a very good tone.

The reason for this is because the sounding quality, or sonorousness of any substance depends upon its hardness and elasticity, and when the head is wet or damp it lacks the necessary hardness, and has not the required elasticity.

Another reason is that when the head is loose and flabby there is not sufficient tension upon the rim to cause it to properly respond to the vibrations of the head, which are much slower than when the head is drawn tight.

What is called a "sharp" tone in the banjo is regulated,

1st. By the tension of the strings, which in all cases regulate its musical pitch.

2d. By the quality, size, tension, elasticity and hardness of the head.

3d. By the size, weight and sonorous qualities of the rim and length of neck. In fact, I might say that

POSITION OF HOLDING THE BANJO FOR STAGE PERFORMANCE ADOPTED BY MANY PLAYERS, KEEPING THE INSTRUMENT AWAY FROM THE BODY.

www.ingramcontent.com/pod-product-compliance
Lightning Source LLC
Chambersburg PA
CBHW031407160426
43196CB00007B/935